A REALLY INCREDIBLE Feast

By Johanna Baldwin

Illustrated by Hannah Wheeler

© Scripture Union 2017
First published 2017

ISBN 978 1 78506 600 9

Scripture Union, Trinity House, Opal Court, Opal Drive, Fox Milne, Milton Keynes,
MK15 0DF, UK
Email: info@scriptureunion.org.uk
Website: www.scriptureunion.org.uk

British Library Cataloguing-in-Publication Data. A catalogue record of this book is
available from the British Library.

Printed and bound in India by Nutech Print Services-India

Scripture Union is an international Christian charity working with
churches in more than 130 countries.

Thank you for purchasing this book. Any profits from this book support SU in
England and Wales to bring the good news of Jesus Christ to children, young
people and families and to enable them to meet God through the Bible and prayer.

Find out more about our work and how you can get involved at:
www.scriptureunion.org.uk (England and Wales)
www.suscotland.org.uk (Scotland)
www.suni.co.uk (Northern Ireland)
www.scriptureunion.org (USA)
www.su.org.au (Australia)

Contents

A super-duper blooper!   4
Jesus turns water into wine (John 2:1–11)

The filthy four and their faith-filled friend   10
Jesus forgives and heals a paralysed man (Luke 5:17–26)

Thrash, crash, splash!   16
Jesus calms the storm (Mark 4:35–41)

Alive and well   20
Jesus raises a dead girl and heals a sick woman (Luke 8:40–56)

It's me, I can see!   26
Jesus heals a blind man (John 9:1–12)

A really incredible feast   30
Jesus feeds the five thousand (Mark 6:1–13)

A Super-Duper Blooper!

A long time ago in a far-away land
A baby was born, who grew into a man ♂
Who said and did some things very odd,
Which made people think he might just be God. ?

Jesus was his name, and he did amazing stuff.
Everywhere he went, people couldn't get enough.
He **healed the unwell,** helped lame people walk,
He gave speech to men who couldn't even talk.

When Jesus was travelling around Galilee,
Preaching and teaching, he stopped to see
His friends getting married, and to join in their feast
With lots and lots of yummy food to eat.

The party was wonderful, splendid, sublime.
The guests were having a fabulous time. ♥
The beautiful bride and the dashing young groom
Laughed with joy as they danced round the room.

The dancing went on, the guests drank more wine,
They drank and drank, then at half past nine,
The wine was all gone, **they'd drunk the whole lot!**
They'd enjoyed it so much, they'd emptied the pots.

The waiters weren't sure what they should do now;
They needed some more but they didn't know how
To find more wine at this time of night
The shops were shut, they knew that was right.

The family would be so ashamed and upset
If there weren't enough drinks for all of their guests.
This could cause chaos, a hullabaloo,
But Jesus' mum Mary knew just what to do!

She sped to her son and told him about
The empty wine pots and the drinks running out.
At first Jesus sounded like he didn't care,
He was still talking with friends who were there.

But Mary was patient, and said they should wait,
"Whatever he tells you, just do it, have faith!"
Mary knew he'd been blessed with great awesome power
From God, his Father – this could be the hour

When people would start to be able to see
What Jesus could do and who he might be.
Eventually Jesus stopped and looked up
As he drained the last of the wine from his cup.

There were six stone jars stood right by the wall,
Gigantic jars, super long and very tall.
Jesus said to the servants, "Now fill them all up
With water as usual, then dip in a cup

So the master can taste it and see what he thinks,
And then all these guests, they can have some more drinks."
The servants were puzzled, but went with the flow;
They wondered just how this could save the show.

6

It seemed like a strange thing to tell them to do,
What was he thinking? None of them knew!
Six jars of water, well what good were they?
They said to themselves "What will master say?"

With six full up jars, they dipped in a cup,
Gave the master a taste, and he started to blush,
"Well this is embarrassing, what a big blooper!
This wine is delicious, it's so super-duper!

You know we should serve the bestest wine first,
The last wine's not good, it should be the worst!
We're meant to start off with the ultimate best,
And after that then work through the rest!

But here's the best wine, saved right up till last!"
The servants, they watched him, faces aghast.
They knew they'd put water in every big jar
But now it was wine, and the best wine by far.

The problem was solved; the party went on.
Mary was proud of her wonderful son.
He'd never done anything like this before,
She had a strange feeling he would do more.

The Filthy Four and their Faith-filled Friend

Luke 5:17-26

"It's good to be back, it's great to see friends. It's nice to sit down at the journey's end.
Some favourite foods and familiar faces. We've travelled so long through so many places."

Jesus was home, and the word soon spread, along with tales of the things he had said,
And the things he had done as he'd travelled around: healings and miracles – in every town.

It sounded amazing – it was hard to know what else he might say, and where he might go.
Everyone wondered what else he might do, and pondered if all they'd heard could be true.

They all came to watch when he started to teach, his friends, their friends and three more each.
Some were lonely, some were sad, some were good and some were bad.

Some came for healing, waiting their turn; some came to argue, some came to learn.
Some were excited, happy and keen; some were grumpy, angry and mean.

Some were young and some were old, some completely broke the mould.
The house was full, the crowd still grew. They gathered around on the outside too.

Jesus looked round at them all with love, and spoke the words of his Father above.
Everyone listened, so keen to hear. They pushed and shoved just to get near.

Just down the road there were eight tired feet, stumbling along and walking the street.
Four weary men, they carried their friend. Surely they must be nearing the end?

The man was lame, **his legs weren't good,** so they carried him through all the dirt and the mud.
In hope and in faith, his friends kept on. They wondered if Jesus might be the one?

But now they were here, the house was crammed. They couldn't get in, the door was jammed!
People were pushing and shoving for space. But there just wasn't room in such a small place!

So **eight aching hands** just put down their mate, and wondered if all they could do was wait.
They puzzled and pondered just what to do now. Surely they had to get in – somehow!

The friends racked their brains: what could they do? They wanted their friend to see Jesus too.
And then it happened, an idea struck. They didn't care about all of the muck!

So four nervous friends, they climbed up top. They'd started now, they couldn't stop.
They carried their friend who was laid out flat, up the stairs, with him and his mat.

On top of the roof they **moved all the tiles,** stacking them up in neat little piles.
After a while there was quite a big hole, and when they looked down they saw Jesus below.

They'd made a huge mess, they'd made a great din. **Filthy they were,** but they'd got a way in.
They lowered him down with a wobble and sway. As he got to the floor people moved out the way.

The man looked around, feeling very unsure. The crowd just stared at their guest on the floor.
Jesus looked down at the man with love, and spoke the words of his Father above.

"Your sins are forgiven, my friend," he said. A little embarrassed, the man turned red.
He thought, "That's amazing, but not why I came. Should I say 'thanks' and go home still lame?"

Everyone stared, they were very confused. They thought through the words that Jesus had used.
The Pharisees, shocked, said "Who is this man? Only God forgives sins! Only he can!"

But Jesus knew just what they thought. They were out to have him caught.
So he said to them, "Is it simpler to say, 'Get up, walk' or 'Your sin's gone away'?"

"I want you to see, my power's from above. It's God who forgives, it's because of his love.
So now I'll say: get up on your feet. Take your mat and go – go home to your street."

The man grabbed his mat, as Jesus had said. He walked down the street with his arm round his bed.
As he walked, he jumped and sang with glee, "Thank you, God, for healing me!"

The crowd was amazed by what they saw. "How can this be?" they said with awe.
Amazed, perplexed, wowed and astounded, they all went home completely dumbfounded.

Thrash, Crash, Splash! Mark 4:35–41

Down by the lake, was Jesus one day,
Crowds super-keen on what he had to say.
His **fishermen friends** were there by his side
But many had come from so far and so wide.

He'd told them **good stories** and taught them ideas,
Brought fresh understanding to all who could hear.
His stories were splendid; they longed to hear more,
He spoke about God like they'd not heard before.

The crowd had grown bigger as more came to watch;
Jesus was starting to feel rather squashed.
His friends found a boat moored up near the shore,
So they jumped in with Jesus and pushed out with oars.

With the boat a short distance away from the crowd,
Jesus kept talking, his voice big and loud.
As he finished his message, the sun headed down,
He sat down to rest and his friends gathered round.

He said, "Let's take the boat and go to that side,"
So inside they climbed and sat down for the ride.
As the shore grew more distant, Jesus grew weary.
He dozed off to sleep as the skies grew more dreary.

The lake was so big, the journey was long,
As they sailed out from shore the winds became strong.
As Jesus did sleep, the wind whirled around,
The waves, they grew bigger and rain hammered down.

The waves **grew** and grew, there was thunder and lightning;
Jesus' friends were finding it frightening.
The waves came crashing and rocking the boat,
Thrashing and splashing, they were barely afloat!

Jesus still slept, on the floor, unaware.
His friends woke him up, shouting, "Lord, don't you care?
We're taking on water, the boat's going down!
We're going to sink; we're going to drown!"

Jesus sat up, a picture of calm,
"What's got you so frightened? We'll come to no harm.
Do you still have no faith, after all that you've seen,
And all that I've taught in the places we've been?"

Then Jesus stood up in the midst of the din,
Stretched out his hands and rebuked the wind.
He spoke to the waves, "Be calm, be at peace,"
And instantly, the storm did cease.

The **wind died down** and the **water was still,**
Their fear went away, they stopped feeling ill,
They looked on at Jesus, still feeling quite dazed,
He stopped the storm, they were oh, so amazed!

They looked at their friend, at the end of the day,
"Who is this man, that the winds do obey?"
They wondered just what was the right thing to say,
"Who is this man, who saved us today?"

Alive and well

When Jesus came home, there were crowds there again,
Loads of them waiting – women, children and men.
Wherever he went, they seemed to come too,
They flocked to his side and even made a queue!

A man named Jairus was there in the throng,
A synagogue man who had come along
To ask for some help in his time of great need;
His 12-year-old girl was very ill indeed.

He'd heard of this man who could heal the sick,
He knew as he left, he'd have to be quick.
His beautiful girl, who had once been so strong,
Was weaker and weaker and might not live long.

Jairus fell at Jesus' feet.
This was the man he'd been rushing to meet.
"Jesus, I need you to come to my place.
My daughter is dying, she's a very bad case.

Jesus, please come and make her OK.
I know that you can, so I'm here today
To ask you to help, please Jesus do.
My daughter, she really, really needs you."

The teacher took pity and went to the house,
Trying to get there unblocked by the crowds.
As the people pressed in, he suddenly stopped,
And turned right around, looking quite shocked.

"Who touched me? Who touched me?" An odd thing to ask,
With crowds really close, it sounded so daft.

"Not me! Not me!" all the people insisted.
But wanting an answer, Jesus persisted.

Peter stepped in, "They **all** touched you, Master,
We need to keep going, could you walk a bit faster?"
But Jesus kept waiting, "Someone touched me, I know.
I felt power leave me, so where did it go?"

At last came an answer: a **woman** fell down
At Jesus' feet, she knelt on the ground.
She had a tale that she wanted to tell;
A tremendous tale that she was not well.

She'd been bleeding and bleeding for 12 long, long years,
Been treated as an outcast, feared other people's sneers.
She'd spent all she had on finding a cure.
Doctors took money, but weren't really sure.

Their remedies were rubbish, they didn't help one bit.
But the woman heard of Jesus, and all that he did,
If she could touch him, or even his cloak,
She knew he could heal her – that was her hope.

So she faced her fears and pushed through the horde,
And the moment she touched him she knew she was cured.
She thought he wouldn't notice, she could just sneak away.
She thought he'd keep walking, and go on his way.

But he knew she had touched him and wanted to know,
Her story, her reasons for touching him so.
And when she turned back and her whole tale was told,
He said, "Go in peace, by faith you're made whole."

While Jesus was still speaking, up ran a man.
For Jairus he'd come, with bad news for their plan.
"I'm so sad to tell you, your daughter has died,
So don't bother Jesus", but Jairus just cried.

His heart was **so sad**, but Jesus said "No!
Don't be afraid; **have faith**, let's go!
She **will be healed**, she will be OK.
Come on, let's go now, keep up, don't delay."

When they arrived, Jesus went on inside.
The parents and friends, they waited outside.
They were **sobbing and wailing**, but Jesus said "Stop!
She's just asleep!" But they knew she was not.

Then Jesus told her, "My child, get up now."
He held her small hand, and she jumped up – Wow!
Her life came straight back, she got up and talked.
Everyone stared as she moved round and walked!

Jesus said, "**Give her food, she needs something to eat.**"
Astonished, and wowed, they turned white as a sheet!
When the girl had her food, Jesus gave them an order.
"**Don't** spread the news that I've raised your daughter."

So Jesus had healed the woman who bled
And then he had raised a young girl from the dead.
To many who asked him, he gave them help too.
I wonder, if asked, **what he might do for you?**

It's me, I can see!

John 9:1–12

Jesus was journeying with his friends, over big hills, and round endless bends.

They walked and talked, they nattered and chattered.

Then Jesus stood still, seeing someone who mattered.

A blind man sat at the side of the street, in raggedy clothes, with big smelly feet.

His eyes didn't work, so he couldn't see. He couldn't get work, or food for tea.

People walked past, like he just wasn't there. But Jesus wasn't like that; Jesus cared.

What came next was really very strange. Jesus didn't give him food, or even spare change.

Jesus crouched down and spat on the ground

And then he put his hand in it and mixed all around!

It was squidgy and squelchy, icky and mucky. Everyone stared and thought it was yucky!

He scooped up some squidge and wiped it upon the man's broken eyes – what was going on?

The man was astonished, astounded, amazed! The people stared, and gawped, and gazed.

"What is he doing? Has he gone mad?" Some of them definitely thought that he had.

But Jesus stayed calm, and said to the man, "Now I want you to walk, so you might need a hand.

"Go to the pool and have a good wash." So the man went off for a splish and a splosh.

He jumped in the pool and washed off the muck, then opened his eyes, and saw a blue duck!

"I can see, I can see! There's a duck, and a tree!" He ran home shouting, "It's me, I can see!"

"It's me, I can see!" the man runs down the street, to the **shock and surprise** of the people he meets.

"Is this the beggar, the man who was blind?" They crowded around him, in front and behind.

"It could be the blind man, but maybe it's Jim, who lives down the road and looks so like him!"

"It's me, it's me! It really is me! I was the blind man, but now I can see!"

The people were shocked – how should they react? If you're blind, you can't see: that is a fact.

Or so they had thought, until that same day, and now they just didn't know what they should say!

"Well, who is this Jesus, and how did he do it?

Get him to tell us, and get him to prove it!"

The people were angry; they thought they'd been tricked.

The man was ecstatic, his problem was fixed!

He wanted them all to share in his joy – the men and the women, the girls and the boys.

So he tried to find **Jesus**, he looked all around, but this strange man Jesus, he couldn't be found.

The people would have to decide what they thought

Of the very strange things Jesus said, did and taught.

Was he a great teacher or just a big pest? Where had he gone? What would he do next?

They wondered if all they had seen could be true. I know what I think, but how about you?

A Really Incredible Feast

John 6:1–13

They'd walked a long way, they needed a break,
So Jesus and friends **sat down by the lake.**
They'd shared the good news while on their way
But now it was time to **eat and pray.**

They needed some **quiet**, some **calm**, some **hush**,
A break from the hustle, the bustle and rush,
But people kept coming and making requests,
How were they meant to **get any rest?**

So then Jesus said, **"Let's go, come with me!"**
And they got in a boat – crossed over the sea.
They landed their boat near fields of green,
They'd made it away from the crowds, unseen.

But **the plan didn't work**, somehow the word spread;
The people found out, so they all ran ahead,
Round the side of the lake to the green grassy field,
With hopes to hear more, or see more healed.

Despite **being tired** and needing to stop,
Jesus didn't grump or get in a strop.
He'd brought his friends here so that they could find space,
But looked on the crowd with **compassion and grace.**

He spoke of God's kingdom, healed those who were ill,
And dealt with all their questions, until
His friends pointed out it was getting quite late,
And maybe, just maybe, it was time that they ate.

"Send the people over there, to find a café
Or a shop or a village and perhaps we may
Then finally find some time to pray
And talk with you by the end of the day."

But Jesus said, "No! Don't send them away;
You find them food, and tell them to stay."
Philip was shocked – an impossible feat!
To find enough food for thousands to eat?

"To earn enough money for all that nosh
It'd take half a year to collect all the dosh.
Besides, just to spend it, well that would be rash.
And anyway, Jesus, we don't have the cash!"

So then Jesus said, "We'll feed the whole lot!
We just need some bread, go and see what we've got!"
"We'll do as you wish," the disciples said,
And found two fish and five loaves of bread.

A young boy had brought them to eat for his tea;
Enough for one, perhaps two, but no more than three.
And absolutely, clearly, there couldn't be a doubt,
Not nearly enough for the crowd who'd turned out.

"Sit everyone down, now that's your task."
Bewildered and baffled, they did as he asked,
In fifties and hundreds, they sat on the ground,
They wondered and watched and looked all around.

"What's going to happen?" some of them mumbled.
They were so hungry their tummies rumbled.
Jesus held up the fish and the bread,
He looked up to heaven, with them overhead.

He said thanks to God and called out aloud,
"Share it all out, feed the whole crowd!"
Peckish and puzzled, the people did stare,
And as the food passed, they took their share.

And right to the last, each and every one,
Munched and crunched and chomped along.
They had their fill of the young boy's tea
Until they were full and smiling with glee.

When everyone had eaten, there were lots of bits
All over the floor, both bread and fish.
The disciples gathered up every last piece
They managed to fill up a basket each!

Twelve baskets filled to the brim with bits,
Five thousand men, plus women and kids,
All were well fed, they'd had plenty to eat,
Jesus fed them all – an incredible feast!